AUDIO ACCESS INCLUDED

DEEP PURPLE

T0061497

PLAYBACK+
Speed • Pitch • Balance • Loop

To access audio visit:
www.halleonard.com/mylibrary

Enter Code
5703-7476-1308-0982

Cover photo: Getty Images/Bob King/Contributor

ISBN 978-1-5400-2975-1

HAL•LEONARD®

Visit Hal Leonard Online at
www.halleonard.com

Contact Us:
Hal Leonard
7777 West Bluemound Road
Milwaukee, WI 53213
Email: info@halleonard.com

In Europe contact:
Hal Leonard Europe Limited
42 Wigmore Street
Marylebone, London, W1U 2RN
Email: info@halleonardeurope.com

In Australia contact:
Hal Leonard Australia Pty. Ltd.
4 Lentara Court
Cheltenham, Victoria, 3192 Australia
Email: info@halleonard.com.au

DEEP PURPLE

CONTENTS

Black Night

Words and Music by Ritchie Blackmore, Ian Gillan,
Roger Glover, Jon Lord and Ian Paice

Intro
Moderate Rock ♩ = 134

%Verse

1. Black night   is not right.
2. See additional lyrics

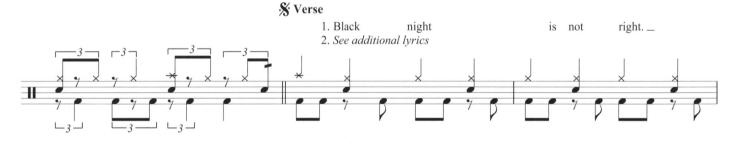

I don't feel   so bright.   Don't care

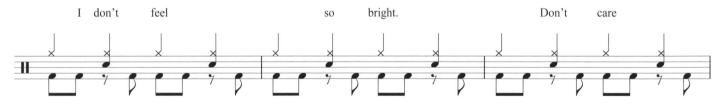

To Coda ⊕

to sit tight. __ May-be I'll find   on the way   down the line that I'm

free,

free _____ to be me.

Black night is a _____ long way from

Interlude

home. _____

D.S. al Coda

Coda

way down the line that I'm

free,

free _____ to be me.

Black night is a _____ long way from

Guitar Solo

home. _____

Play 7 times

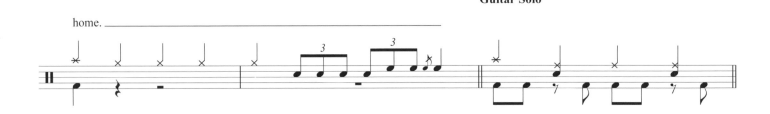

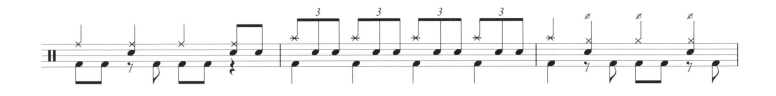

Organ Solo

6

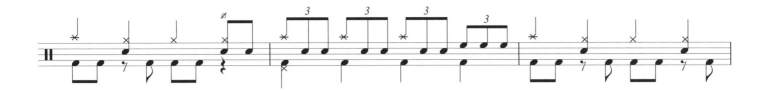

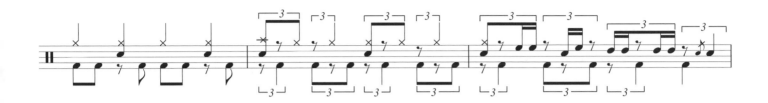

Verse

3. Black   night,   black   night.

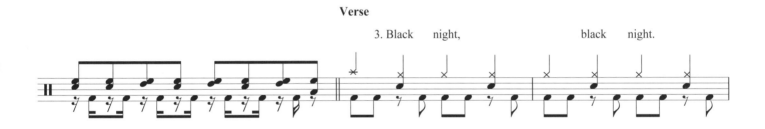

I don't   need   black   night.   I can't see ___

dark   light.   May - be I'll find   all the way down the line that I'm

Outro-Guitar Solo

Additional Lyrics

2. Don't need a dark tree.
   I don't want a rough sea.
   I can't feel; I can't see.
   Maybe I'll find all the way down the line that I'm free,
   Free to be me.
   Black night is a long way from home.

Fireball

Words and Music by Ritchie Blackmore, Ian Gillan,
Roger Glover, Jon Lord and Ian Paice

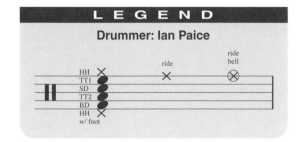

Intro

Fast Rock ♩ = 240

Verse

1. The gold - en light a - bove _

___ you will show me where you're from. _____ The

mag - ic in your eye _____ be - witch - es all ___ you gaze up - on. ___

___ You stand up on your hill; _____ they

be - bop all a - round ___ you. They won - der where you're from, ___

___ oh, yeah. They won - der where I found ___ you.

Chorus

Oh, my love, _____ it's a _____ long way. _____

___ Where you're from, _____ it's a ___

___ long way. _____

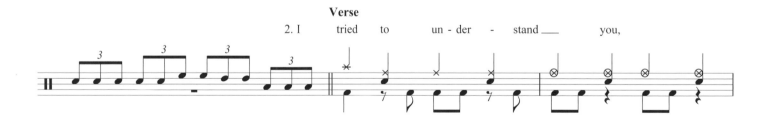

Verse

2. I tried to un - der - stand ___ you,

tried to love you right. ___ The way you smile and touch ___

Bridge

Mag - ic wom - an wreck - in' up __

__ my soul. __ Things __ you tell me __ have

__ nev - er been told. Mag - ic

wom - an, __ I __ don't know. __ E -

lec - tric be - fore me, __ I love you so, I love __

__ you so. Oh, __ whoa. __

Verse

__ 3. You're rac - ing like a fire -

Chorus

long   way.

Bass Solo

Interlude

Organ Solo

Verse

4. The gold - en light a - bove ___ you, _____

show me where you're from. ___ The mag - ic in your eye _

___ be - witch - es all ___ you gaze up - on. ___ You

stand   up   on your   hill, _____   be - bop   all   a - round_

_____   you.   They won - der   where you're   from, ____   oh,   yeah,   they

Chorus

won - der   where I   found ____ you. _____   Oh,   my

love, _____   it's   a _____   long   way. _____

Where   you're   from, _____   it's   a _____   long   way. _____

Outro

Begin fade

Fade out

Highway Star

Words and Music by Ritchie Blackmore, Ian Gillan,
Roger Glover, Jon Lord and Ian Paice

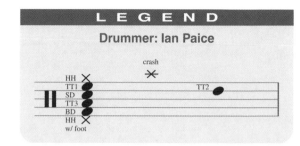

A no - bod - y gon - na beat my car, __ it's gon - na break the speed of sound. _____
A no - bod - y gon - na steal my head, now that I'm on the road a - gain. _____

2nd time, substitute Fill 1

Ooh, __ it's a kill - in' ma - chine, _ it's got a ev - 'ry - thing. __
Ooh, __ I'm in heav - en a - gain, _ I got a ev - 'ry - thing. __

2nd time, substitute Fill 2

Like a driv - in' pow - er, big fat tires __ and ev - 'ry - thing. __
Like a mov - in' ground, __ an o - pen road __ and ev - 'ry - thing.

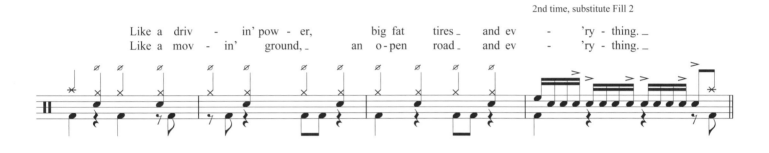

𝄋 𝄋 **Chorus**

1., 3. I love __ it! And I need __ it! I bleed __ it!
2. I love __ her! I need __ her! I feel __ it!

Fill 1

Fill 2

19

Yeah, _ it's a wild _ hur-ri-cane!
Eight cyl-in-ders, all _ mine!

All _____ right! _____ Hold _

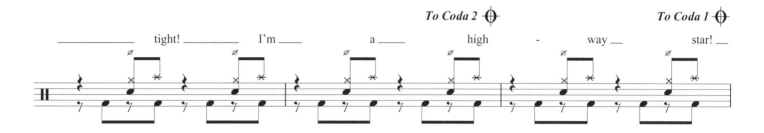

_____ tight! _____ I'm _____ a _____ high - way _ star! _

To Coda 2 ⊕ *To Coda 1* ⊕

Verse

2. No - bod - y gon-na take my girl, _ I'm gon-na keep her to the end. _____

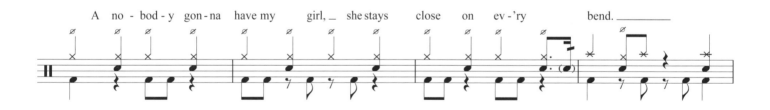

A no - bod - y gon-na have my girl, _ she stays close on ev-'ry bend. _____

Ooh, _____ she's a kill-in' ma-chine, _ she's got a ev-'ry-thing. _

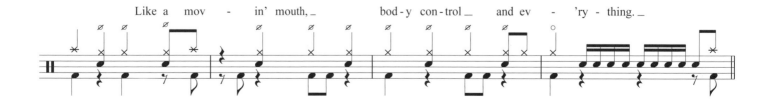

Like a mov - in' mouth, _ bod-y con-trol _ and ev-'ry-thing. _

Chorus

I love __ her!   And I need __ her!   I see __ her!

Yeah, __ she turns __ me on!   All __ right! __ Hold __

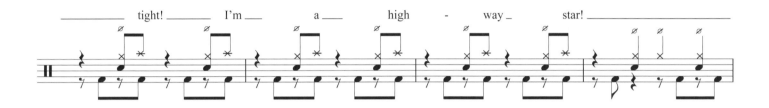

__ tight! __ I'm __ a __ high - way __ star! __

Keyboard Solo

22

Coda 1

Guitar Solo

Verse

4. No - bod - y gon - na take my car, __ I'm gon - na race it to the ground. __

A no - bod - y gon - na beat my car, __ it's gon - na break the speed of

sound. _____ Ooh, _____ it's a kill - in' ma - chine, __

it's got a ev - 'ry - thing. ___   Like a driv -

D.S.S. al Coda 2

- in' pow - er,   big fat tires ___ and ev - 'ry - thing. ___

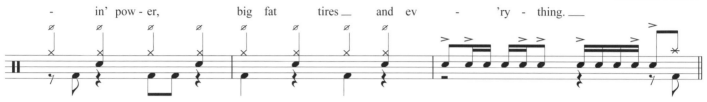

⊕ Coda 2

- way ___ star! ___   I'm ___ a ___ high - way ___

___ star! ___   I'm ___ a ___ high - way ___

Free time
star!

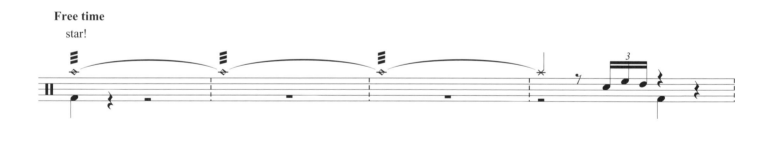

buzz
roll

rit.

Knocking at Your Back Door

Words and Music by Ritchie Blackmore, Ian Gillan and Roger Glover

Pre-Chorus

Chorus

Guitar Solo

3. Sweet _____

Verse

Lu - cy was a danc - er, but none of us ___ would chance her, be - cause she was a sam - u - rai. ___

___ She made e - lec - tric shad - ows ___ be - yond ___ our fin - ger - tips, and

Interlude

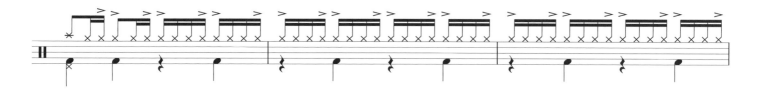

Ah, _

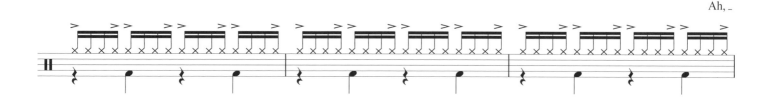

_ ha, knock-ing at your back door. _____

Outro-Guitar Solo

Begin fade

Fade out

Perfect Strangers

Words and Music by Ritchie Blackmore, Ian Gillan and Roger Glover

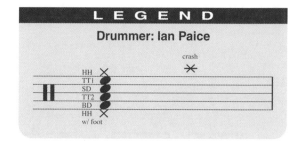

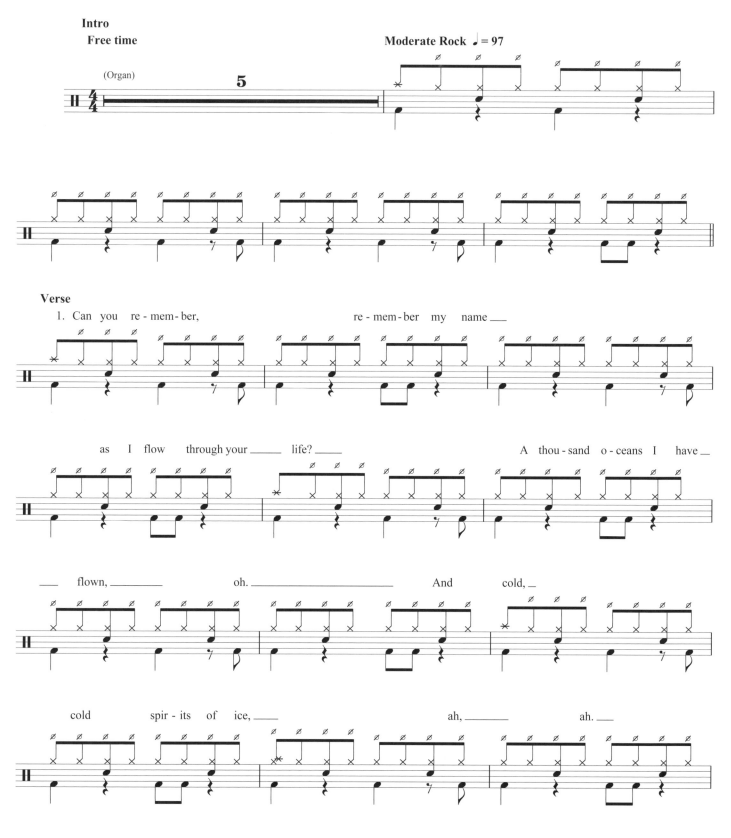

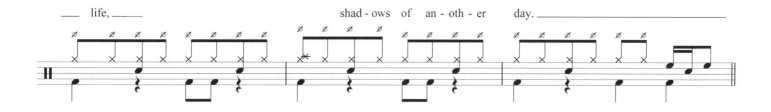

shad - ows of an - oth - er day. _____

Chorus

And if you hear me talk - ing on the wind, you've got to

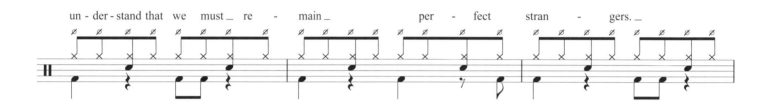

un - der - stand that we must __ re - main __ per - fect stran - gers. __

Interlude

Ah, ____ la, __ la, ____ la, ____ oo. __

I know I

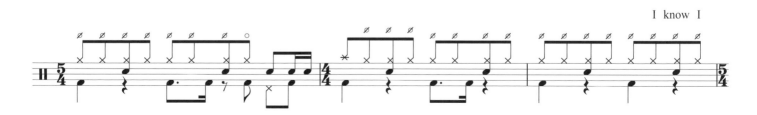

must re-main in - side this si - lent well of sor - row.

Verse

3. A strand of sil - ver

hang - ing through the sky, touch - ing more than _ you

see; the voice of ag - ges in your mind, oh, _

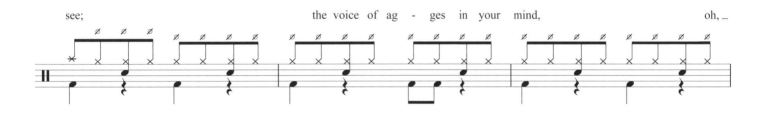

_____ is ach - ing____ with the dead of the night. _

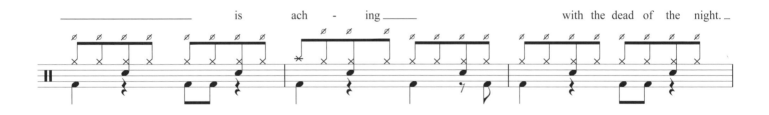

_ Oh, _____ oh, ____

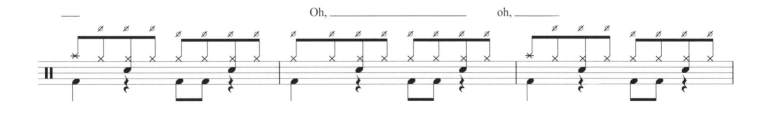

pre - cious life, _ your tears are lost in fall - ing rain. _____

39

Chorus

And if you hear me talk - ing on the wind, you've got to

un - der-stand we must __ re - main __ per - fect stran - gers. __

Outro

40

Begin fade

Fade out

Smoke on the Water

Words and Music by Ritchie Blackmore, Ian Gillan,
Roger Glover, Jon Lord and Ian Paice

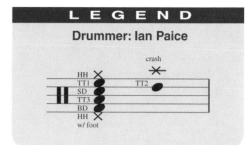

Intro
Moderate Rock ♩ = 112

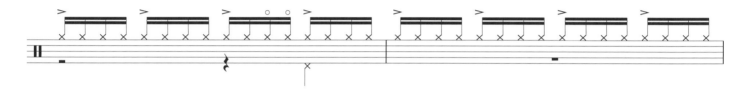

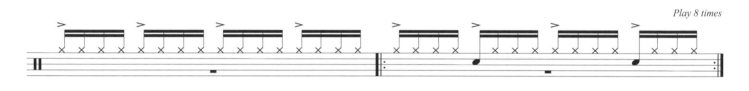

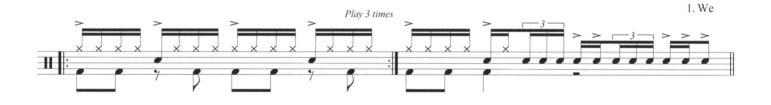

Verse

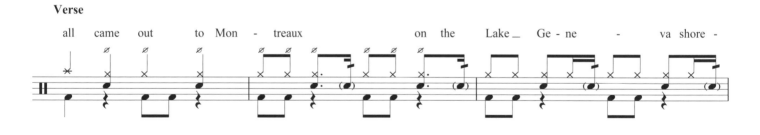

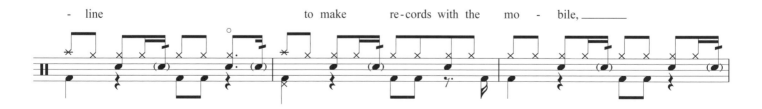

we did-n't have much time. _ But Frank Zap-pa and the

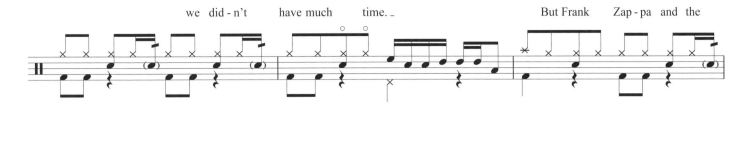

Moth - ers _____ were at the best place a - round. _

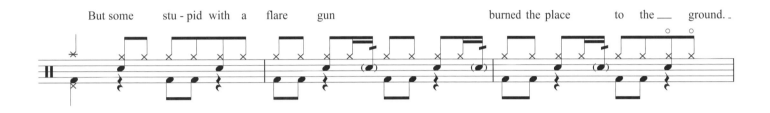

But some stu - pid with a flare gun burned the place to the __ ground. _

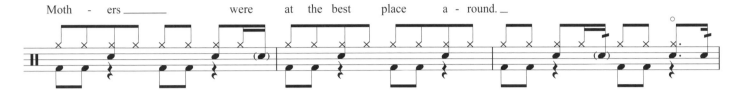

Chorus

Smoke on the wa - ter,

a fire __ in the sky. _ Smoke on the

wa - ter.

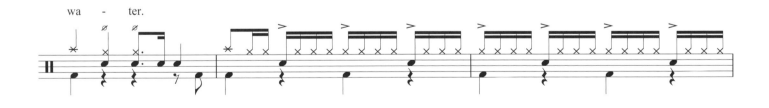

Verse

2. They burned down the gam - bling house, __ it died with an aw - ful sound. __

__ A Funk - y Claude was run - ning in and out, __

pull - ing kids out the ground. __ When it all was o -

- ver, __ we had to find an - oth - er place. __

But Swiss time was run - ning out; it seemed that we would lose the race. __

Chorus

__ Smoke on the wa - ter,

44

a fire ___ in the sky. ___   Smoke   on the

wa - ter.   *Play 6 times*

Guitar Solo

Play 6 times

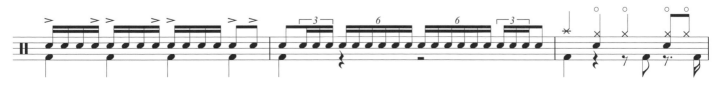

45

Play 6 times

Verse

3. We end - ed up at the Grand Ho - tel, _____ it was emp - ty,

cold and bare. But with the Roll - ing truck Stones thing just out - side,

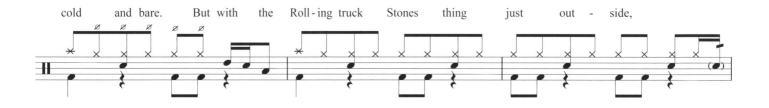

mak - ing our mu - sic there. _ With a few red lights, a

few old beds _ we made a place to sweat. _

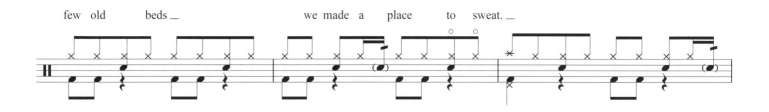

No mat - ter what we get out of this, I know, I know we'll

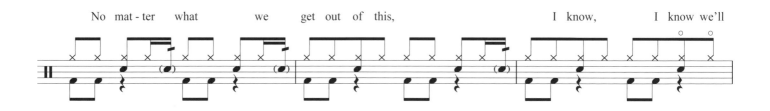

never for-get.

Chorus

Smoke　　　　on　the　wa　-　ter,

a　fire ___ in　the　sky. ___　　　　　　　　　　　　　　　　　Smoke　　　　on　the

wa　-　ter.

Outro

Play 7 times

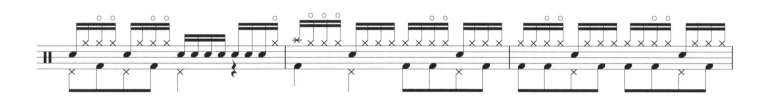

Play 7 times　　　　　　　　　　　　　　　　　　　　　　　　*Play 3 times*

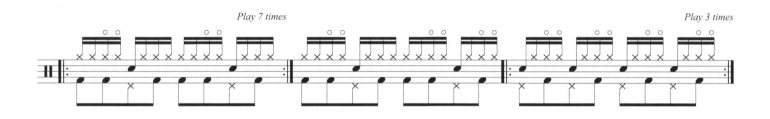

Begin fade

Fade out

Space Truckin'

Words and Music by Ritchie Blackmore, Ian Gillan,
Roger Glover, Jon Lord and Ian Paice

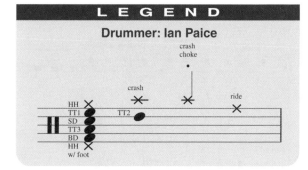

Drummer: Ian Paice

Intro
Moderate Rock ♩ = 129

(Organ & Bass)

Verse

1. Well, __ we had a lot of luck on Ve - nus. We

al - ways had a ball on Mars. __ We're meet - in' all the groov - y peo -

ple. We fight the Milk - y Way so far. ____ We

danced a - round A - bor - e - al - is. We're space truck - in' 'round the stars. __

Chorus

Come on! Come

on! Come on! Let's go space truck - in'. Come

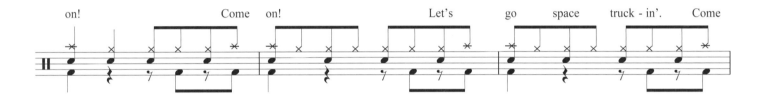

on! Come on! Come on!

Verse

Space truck - in'. 2. Re - mem - ber when we did the moon __ shot and

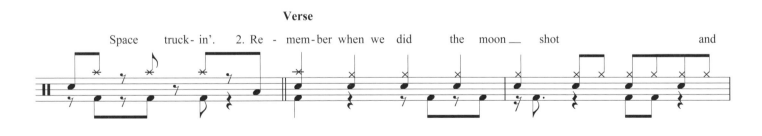

pon - y trek - er led the way. ____ We moved to look at men in the moon __

_____ stuff, and ev-'ry-one be-gan to sway. _____ Got

mu - sic in our so - lar sys - tem. We're space truck-in' 'round the stars. _____

Chorus

Come on! Come

on! Come on! Let's go space truck - in'. Come

on! Come on! Come on!

Bridge

Space truck - in'. The fel - low that we brought was mov - ing, but

now we got a new ma - chine. _____ Yeah, yeah, _ yeah, _

Guitar Solo

Space truck-in'.

Drum Solo

*Overdubbed drum break. (Snares off, next 17 meas.)

**Play with one stick while other stick presses into head to deaden and raise pitch.

52

Interlude

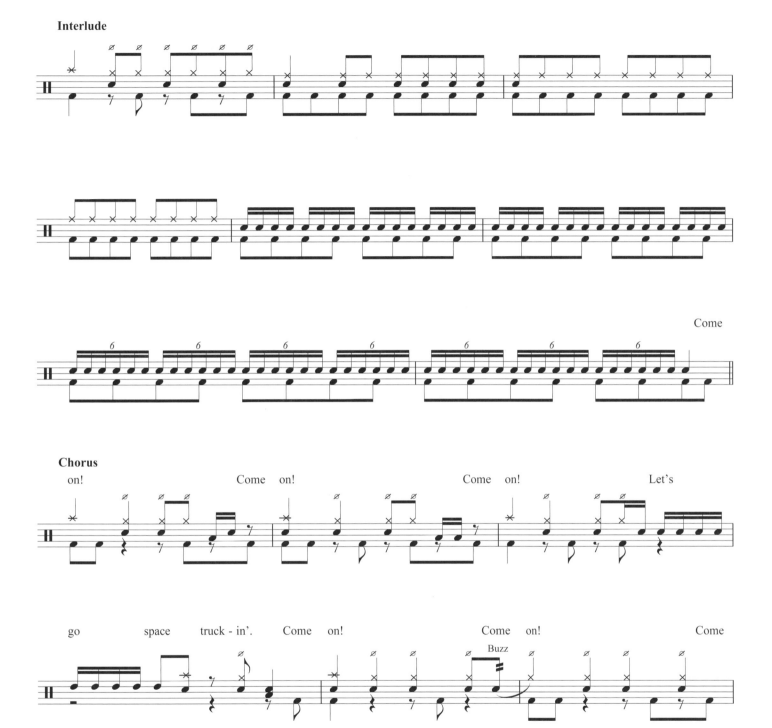

Come

Chorus

on!   Come   on!   Come   on!   Let's

go   space   truck - in'.   Come   on!   Come   on!   Come

Outro

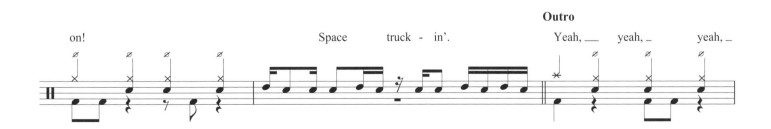

on!   Space   truck - in'.   Yeah, __   yeah, _   yeah, _ space truck - in'. Yeah, ____ yeah, ___ yeah, ____ space truck - in'.

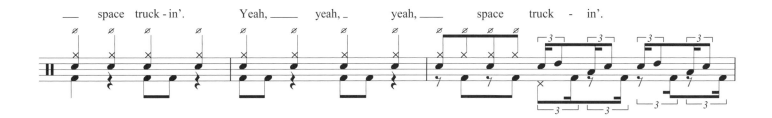

Yeah, ___ yeah, ___ yeah, ____ space truck - in'. Yeah, yeah, ___ yeah, ____

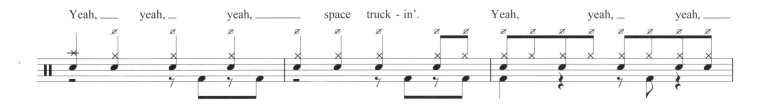

____ yeah, yeah, yeah. Yeah, ___ yeah, ___ yeah, ____ space truck - in'.

Buzz

Yeah, _____ yeah, yeah.

$(\text{♫} = \text{♫})$

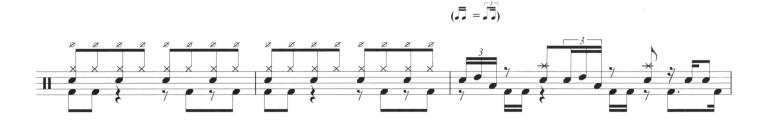

Begin fade

Fade out

Woman from Tokyo

Words and Music by Ritchie Blackmore, Ian Gillan,
Roger Glover, Jon Lord and Ian Paice

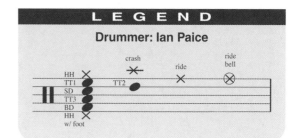

Intro

Moderate Rock ♩ = 126

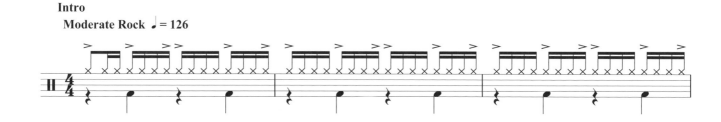

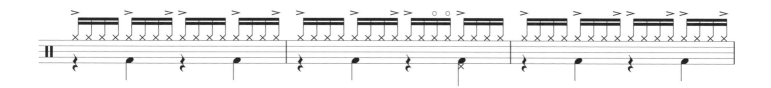

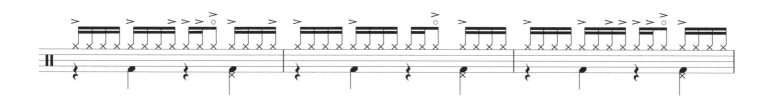

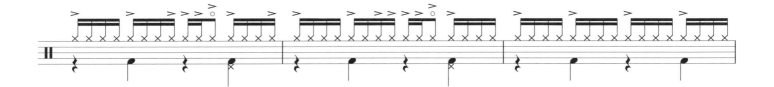

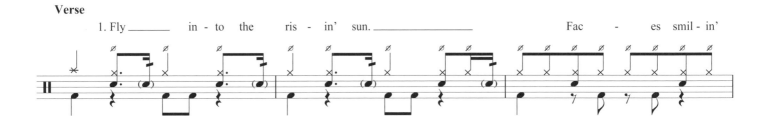

Verse

1. Fly _____ in - to the ris - in' sun. _____ Fac - es smil - in'

ev - 'ry - one. _____ Yeah! She is a whole new tra - di - tion. Ow! __

Chorus

___ I feel it in my heart. _____ My wom - an from To -

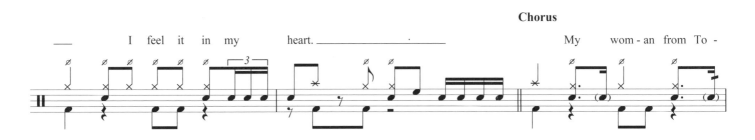

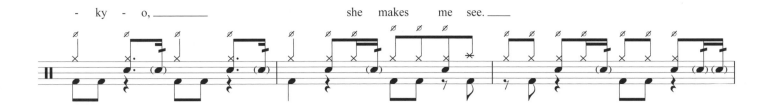

Verse

Chorus

uh, she's so good to ___ me. ___ But I'm at home and I,

I just don't ___ be - long. ___

Bridge

So far ___ a -

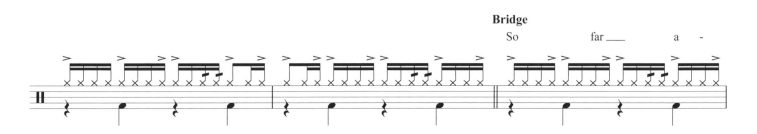

way from ___ the gar - den ___ we love. ___

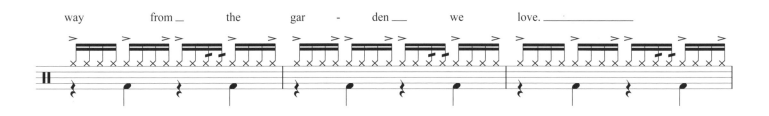

She is ___ what moves ___ in the

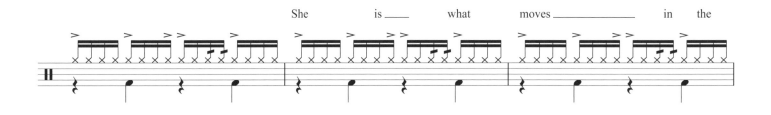

soul of ___ a dove.

Oo. ___

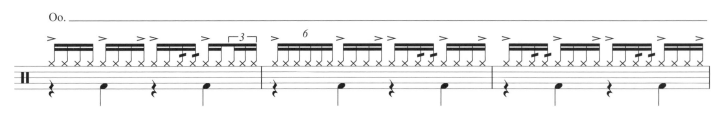

Soon I ___ shall

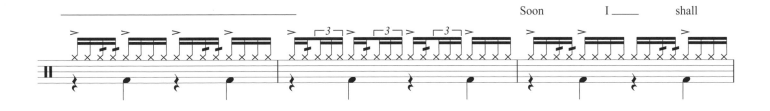

see just ___ how black was ___ my night, _____

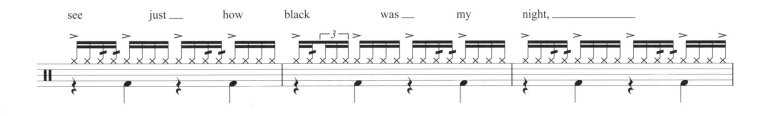

when we're ___ a - lone _____ in her

cit - y ___ of light.

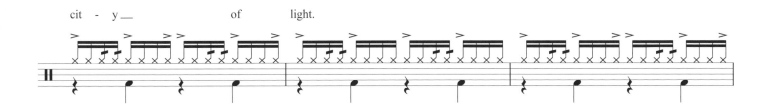

Oo. _____

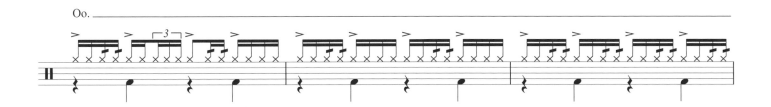

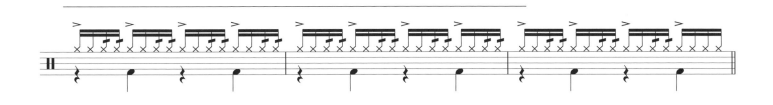

Interlude

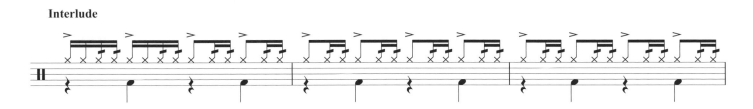

Verse

3. Ris - in' from the ne - on gloom, _____

shin - in' like a cra - zy moon. _____ Yeah, she turns me

Chorus

Interlude

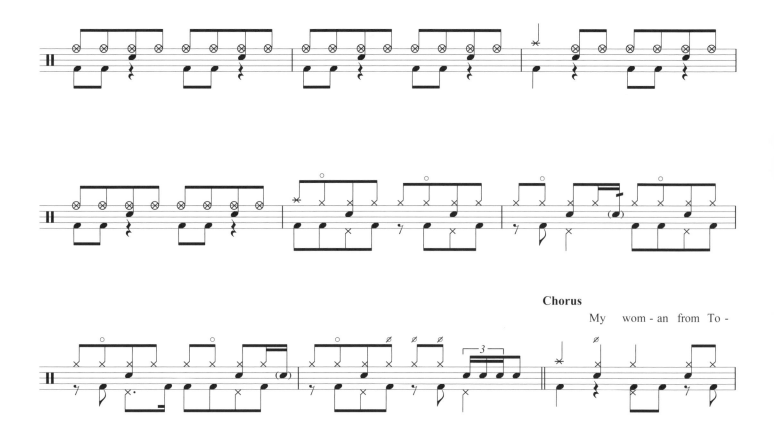

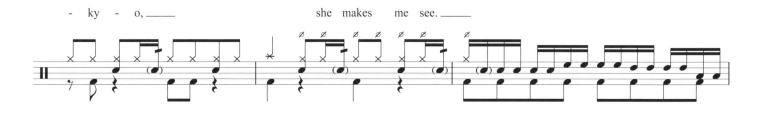

Chorus

My wom-an from To-

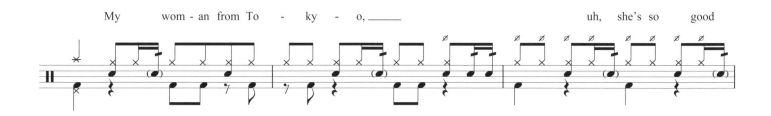

- ky - o, _____ she makes me see. _____

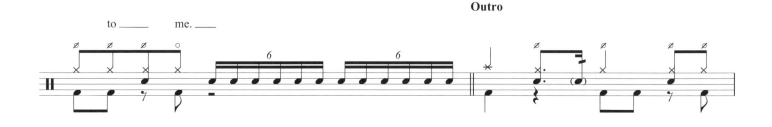

My wom-an from To - ky - o, _____ uh, she's so good

Outro

to _____ me. _____

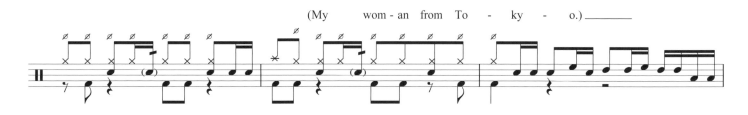

(My wom-an from To - ky - o.) _____

Begin fade

Fade out

HAL•LEONARD®
DRUM PLAY-ALONG

AUDIO ACCESS INCLUDED

The Drum Play-Along™ Series will help you play your favorite songs quickly and easily! Just follow the drum notation, listen to the audio to hear how the drums should sound, and then play-along using the separate backing tracks. The lyrics are also included for reference. The audio files are enhanced so you can adjust the recording to any tempo without changing pitch!

HAL•LEONARD®
Visit Hal Leonard Online at
www.halleonard.com

1218
301

Prices, contents and availability subject to change without notice and may vary outside the US.